Little Eco Experts

Ways to Recycle

Translated by
Diana Osorio

How to be guardians of the planet

PowerKiDS press

Published in 2023 by PowerKids, an Imprint of Rosen Publishing
29 East 21st Street, New York, NY 10010

Cataloging-in-Publication Data
Names: Editorial Sol 90 (Firm).
Title: Ways to recycle / by the editors at Sol90.
Description: New York : Powerkids Press, 2023. | Series: Little eco experts | Includes glossary and index.
Identifiers: ISBN 9781725337008 (pbk.) | ISBN 9781725337022 (library bound) | ISBN 9781725337015 (6pack) | ISBN 9781725337039 (ebook)
Subjects: LCSH: Recycling (Waste, etc.)--Juvenile literature. | Renewable natural resources--Juvenile literature. | Environmental responsibility--
Juvenile literature.
Classification: LCC TD794.5 W397 2023 | DDC 333.7--dc23

Coordination: Nuria Cicero
Editor: Alberto Hernández
Editor, Spanish: Diana Osorio
Layout: Àngels Rambla
Design Adaptation: Raúl Rodriguez, R studio T, NYC
Project Team: Vicente Ponce, Rosa Salvía, Paola Fornasaro
Scientific Advisory Services: Teresa Martínez Barchino

Imaging and Infographics:
www.infographics90.com
Photo Sources: Getty/Thinkstock, AGE Fotostock, Cordon Press/Corbis, Shutterstock.

Manufactured in the United States of America

CPSIA Compliance Information: Batch #CSPK23. For Further Information contact Rosen Publishing, New York, New York at 1-800-237-9932.

CONTENTS

WHAT IS RECYCLING?

Recycling is separating out waste—paper, cardboard, metal, plastic, glass, and organic matter—and reusing it or transforming it into new products.

If we recycle and make use of waste, we improve the environment because we save raw materials and energy.

This is the symbol of recycling.

The amount of waste generated is one of the greatest problems for the environment. We must reduce this quantity and recycle what we can.

90% of household waste can be recycled

WHY RECYCLING IS GOOD

It Decreases Pollution

In addition to reducing the volume of garbage, recycling prevents buildup in landfills, which generates substances that pollute the air.

It Saves Natural Resources

Trees take many years to grow. Therefore, by recycling paper, we can prevent more trees from being cut down, and thus, deforestation.

It Saves Energy

Far more energy is spent extracting and manufacturing new materials than recycling them.

DID YOU KNOW?

Thanks to recycling, we can fight the destruction of the environment. We make materials last longer, and, by doing so, we can live in a cleaner world.

It takes a great deal of energy to manufacture glass and glass products.

Aluminum is a very common metallic element. Cans and food packaging are made from it. It is 100 percent reusable.

Plastic comes from petroleum (oil). Recycling plastic means extracting less petroleum, which can be a polluting substance.

When we recycle paper, we reduce the number of trees being cut down. Paper production also uses water and energy.

CURIOUS FACTS

See what can be done with some recycled materials...

670

Metal Cans

=

Bicycle

27
Plastic
Bottles

=

Waterproof
Jacket

DID YOU KNOW?

It's a problem if we waste too much paper—especially if we do not recycle afterward.

1 Tree

=

Paper

165 pounds (75 kg)

=

12,500

Sheets of Paper

Paper is manufactured from the wood pulp of trees.

Look at these interesting facts about paper and its use:

One person wastes about 650 pounds (295 kg) of paper a year.

But most of this paper can be recycled. This prevents more trees from being cut down.

HOW TO RECYCLE PAPER

Paper products include newspapers, sheets, envelopes, boxes, and cardboard.

It is rolled up on spools.

The result is pressed and dried to make paper.

It is collected in a container, often blue, meant for paper.

First, it is sorted and chopped up.

Paper pulp is manufactured from it.

WHY PAPER NEEDS TO BE RECYCLED

Prevents the Felling of Trees

It prevents trees from being cut down for paper.

Reduces Waste

It reduces the amount of waste generated from paper being thrown out.

Reduces Energy Consumption

Recycling paper reduces energy consumption compared to manufacturing paper directly from wood from trees.

More Recycled Paper Means More:

toilet paper,
bags,
envelopes,
cat litter,
and much more!

HOW CAN WE RECYCLE PLASTIC?

Plastic products include bottles, bags, jugs, tubs, and containers.

New plastic containers are manufactured.

Plastic becomes granulated.

Plastic is collected in special containers.

The contents are separated by types of plastic.

These are washed and crushed separately.

WHY PLASTIC NEEDS TO BE RECYCLED

It Prevents Garbage Accumulation

Recycling plastic pollutes less and prevents the buildup of garbage.

What can be produced with recycled plastic:

toys,
chairs,
cutlery,
plates,
glasses,
bags,
bottles,
and much more!

It Saves Natural Resources

Natural resources, such as petroleum, are saved if plastic is reused or recycled.

It Saves Energy

Energy is saved because recycling plastic requires less energy than fabricating plastic from raw materials.

Separate plastic by types.

This cap is made with one type of plastic. The bottle is made with a different type.

HOW TO RECYCLE GLASS

Glass products include bottles, glasses, jars, and containers.

New containers are manufactured.

Glass is collected in special containers.

It is melted in a glass factory.

WHY GLASS NEEDS TO BE RECYCLED

Glass is one of the easiest materials to recycle. It can be melted at very high temperatures and, once melted, it can be reused.

It Is Very Easy to Recycle!

Curious Fact

Four recycled bottles save the electricity needed to keep a refrigerator running all day.

Glass is totally recyclable.

It Is 100% Recyclable!

Recycling glass saves consumption of many of the materials that compose it and a significant amount of energy. Why is that? Lower temperatures are required to melt waste glass than to manufacture glass from raw materials.

It Reduces Energy and Materials

WHY METAL NEEDS TO BE RECYCLED

Metal is a natural resource extracted from mines. Steel and aluminum are different types of metals. If we recycle them, we reduce the amount of extracted raw materials.

It Reduces the Extraction of Raw Materials

Recycling Process

Metal objects are shredded and melted to be able to reuse the metal. In order to separate the metals from other materials that make up the product, a large magnet is used to attract the metals.

Steel is completely recyclable and can be recycled an unlimited number of times, without losing quality.

It Can Be Recycled Unlimitedly Without Losing Quality

Curious Fact

Some paper containers have a layer of aluminum, which can be separated from the other materials.

SPECIAL MATERIALS

For other kinds of waste, there are places that collect used furniture, appliances, iron, wood, and more...

Tires

These are made of rubber. They can be crushed and used to make pipes.

Electrical Devices

If they still work, they can be given to an organization that will send them to those who need them. If they are broken, they can be recycled to make other devices.

Look for special containers in which to place batteries, used cooking oil, light bulbs, and other materials you would like to recycle.

Oil, Ink, and Paints

These are very difficult to recycle. It is best to use a printer with refillable ink cartridges.

Batteries

They cannot be thrown away because they contain toxic substances. It is best to use rechargeable batteries.

RECYCLE

WHAT CAN YOU DO?

To reduce the amount of garbage we produce, it is important to follow these 4 recycling rules. Turn the page, and read them!

Recycle

If we separate the waste we generate ourselves, we make it easier for the waste to be given a new use.

Recover

This consists of recovering materials or elements that serve as raw materials. For example, different metals can be recovered from cans. That is why it is important to recycle them.

Reuse

Many things that end up in the trash could be reused. We can give things we no longer use, such as clothes or even toys, to people in need.

Reduce

Do not buy things that will become garbage. If you are going to buy something, bring a reusable shopping bag. We can also save paper by reading a document on a computer screen, without printing it.

DO YOU KNOW HOW PAPER IS MADE?

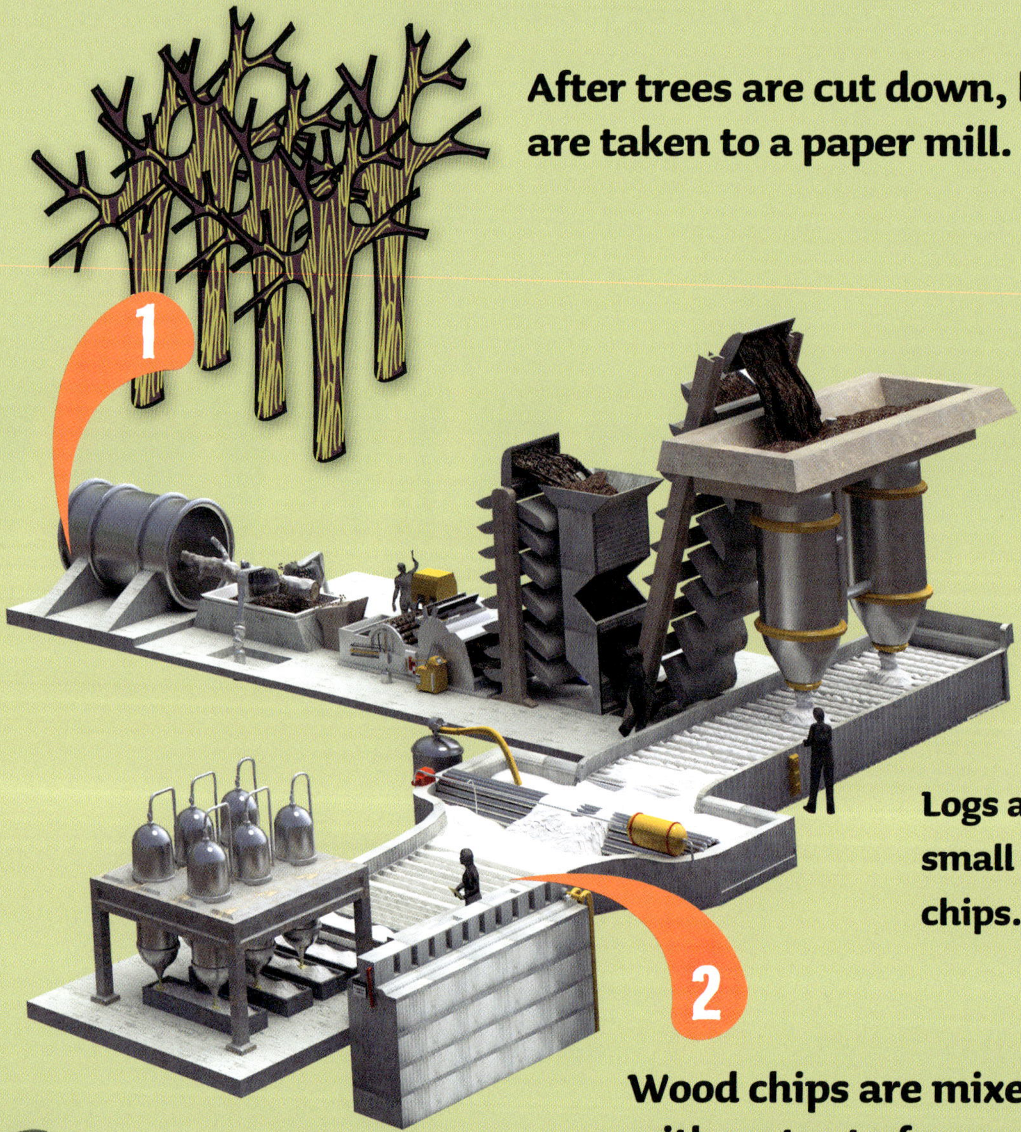

After trees are cut down, logs are taken to a paper mill.

Bark is removed from the tree trunks. Bark does not make good paper.

Logs are cut into small bits or chips.

Wood chips are mixed with water to form a pulp.

The pulp is passed through a machine where it is pressed into large sheets of paper.

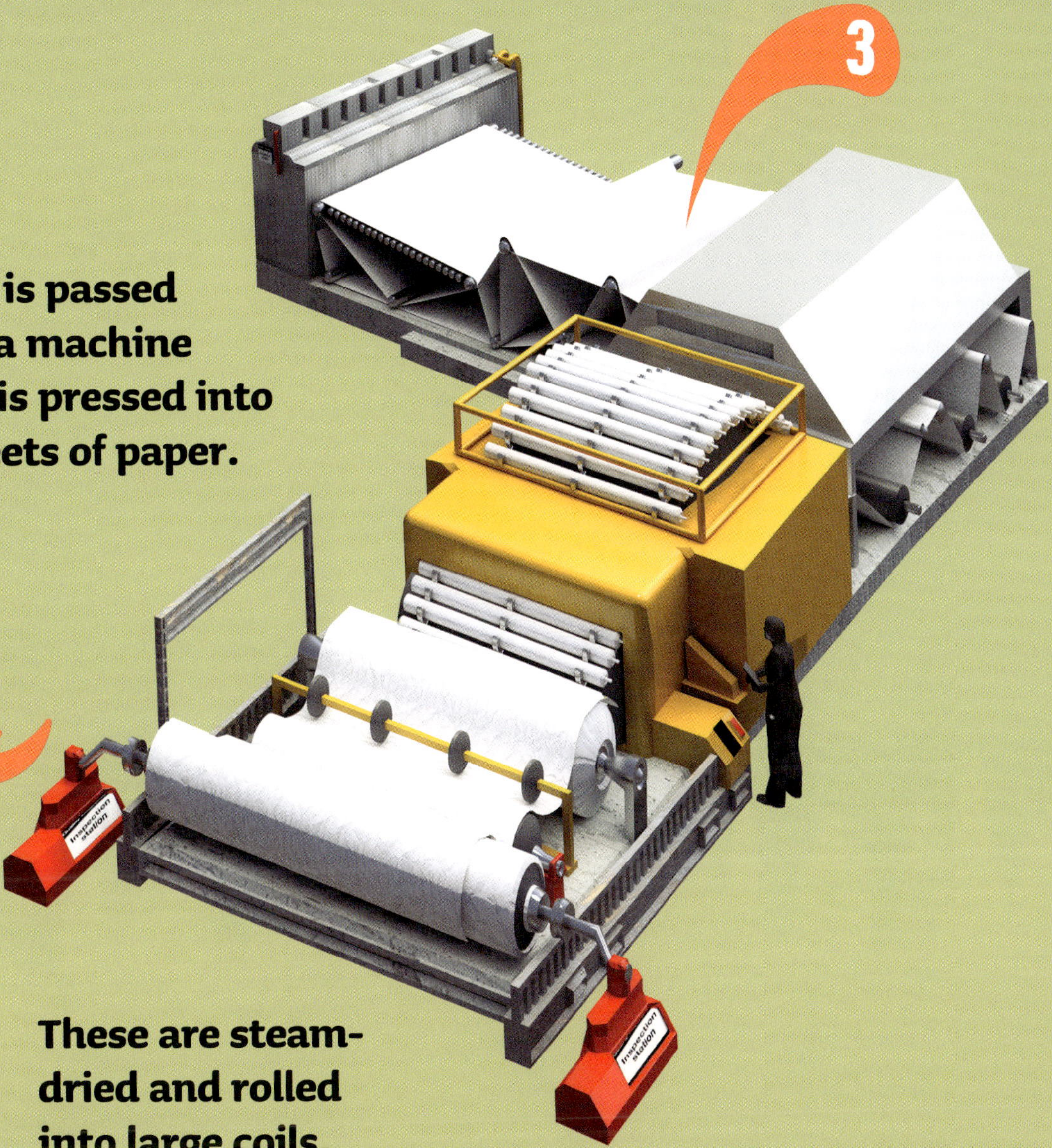

These are steam-dried and rolled into large coils.

RECYCLE PAPER AT HOME

There is no secret about making paper, and it allows you to recycle. Let's go!

YOU WILL NEED:
- **Newspapers**
- **Paper you want to throw out**
- **Water**
- **Blender**
- **Large rectangular container**
- **Sheets of nylon or wire mesh**
- **Spatula**
- **Rolling pin**

OPTIONAL: coloring • dried peppermint or cinnamon • cornstarch

STEP BY STEP: Find the instructions on the next page.

STEP ONE

Cut paper into small pieces, and place inside the blender with a cup of water. Grind everything well, and you have paper pulp!

STEP TWO

You can give the pulp color and smell by adding coloring and spices. To make it shine, add cornstarch.

STEP THREE

Put several sheets of newspaper in the bottom of the container.

STEP FOUR

Spread one of the meshes on the newspaper sheets and spread the paper pulp on top.

STEP FIVE

Cover the pulp with the other mesh and more sheets of newspaper. Roll it with a rolling pin to spread it well.

6

STEP SIX

Take out the paper carefully, and remove the sheets of newspaper and the mesh. Dry it in the sun, and that's it!

Glossary

consumption: the use of a material

element: the most basic part of something

extraction: the process of taking a metal out of an ore. Also, the process of withdrawing a substance from another through a chemical or physical action.

felling: cutting down a tree

granulated: having the form of grains or small particles

manufacture: to make something using raw materials

mine: a pit or tunnel in the ground from which minerals are taken out of the earth

organic: describing something that came from a living organism

pulp: a soft matter that is made mostly from wood which is used in making paper

Index